7 WEST
THROUGH THE
Blue Ridge

CLARE REED

author HOUSE®

AuthorHouse™
1663 Liberty Drive
Bloomington, IN 47403
www.authorhouse.com
Phone: 833-262-8899

Published by AuthorHouse 11/23/2020

ISBN: 978-1-7283-5165-0 (sc)
ISBN: 978-1-7283-5163-6 (e)

Print information available on the last page.

The publication team would like to thank the following people and businesses for their invaluable assistance:

Bruce Clark	*Guitar Transcription*	*All songs*
Keyboard Adventures, Purcellville, VA	*Piano Transcription*	*7 West Through The Blue Ridge* *Only Yesterday*
Music Rx, Marietta, GA	*Piano Transcription*	*Forever Yours* *Jesus, I Love You Most Of All* *Just A Step Away* *Pickles and Bubblegum* *Teardrops*
Terry Hale	*Editor*	*Project Coordination*

Welcome!

Welcome to Clare Reed's journey through the Blue Ridge Mountains of Virginia! Seven original songs and more than 50 pictures from the towns along Route 7 from Leesburg to Winchester are a gift from Clare to friends and newcomers alike.

Many of us know Clare's music from church, bluegrass bands, the Round Hill jam, musicals, and other venues. Join us in celebrating Clare's music and memories of -

7 West Through The Blue Ridge!

Table of Contents

About Route 7

Route 7 is an old rural highway in extreme northern Virginia. Although it runs from Alexandria at the edge of the Potomac River to Winchester on the west side of the Blue Ridge mountains, the interesting part goes from Leesburg to Winchester. It has physical beauty, historic towns, the occasional old-time restaurant or hardware store, and people who are trying to live their lives the right way regardless of their circumstances.

Here's where it's located. See the northern tip of Virginia? No, farther north. Keep going. Look at the faint line going east out of Winchester. The state map shows Route 7 crossing the Blue Ridge Mountains. The inset maps show the detailed views, including the towns pictured or mentioned in the songs. It's a worthwhile journey!

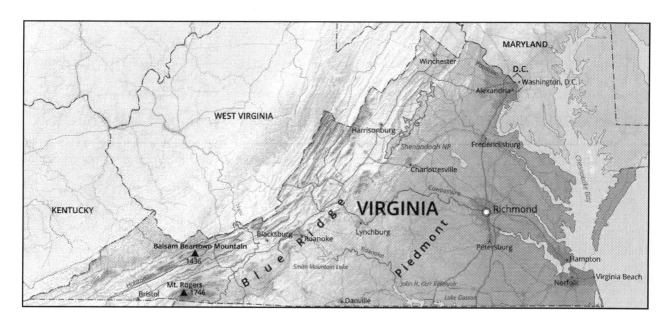

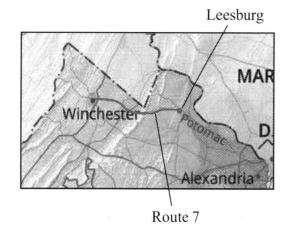

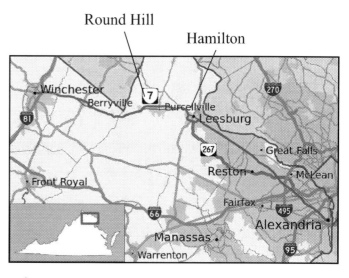

"7 West Through The Blue Ridge"

Words and Music by Clare Reed 1995

1

7 West Through The Blue Ridge

Verse 1:
     C
I'm headed 7 West through the Blue Ridge.

                              G
I'm watchin' Fall leaves fallin' town to town.
I smell the wood stoves burnin' in the valley

                         C
And I know that I am homeward bound.

Verse 2:
     C
I know their still servin' breakfast at the Pine Grove

                             G
And that the Bluemont Fair is comin' 'round.
I see the sun a settin' o're the Blue Ridge.

                      C
There's no prettier sight to be found.

Bridge:
          F   *C*
I'm headed home to see my baby.

        F   *C*
I'm gonna kiss and hold him tight.

      F   *C*
I've put a lot of road behind me.

   D   *G*
But, I'm gonna be there tonight.

Verse 3:
     C
It's been three long weeks since I've been home

                   G
And it feels like months to me.
But the road's getting shorter and it won't be long

                      C
I'll be reachin' in my pocket for my key.

Verse 1:
     C
I'm headed 7 West through the Blue Ridge.

                           G
Im watchin' Fall leaves fallin' town to town.
I smell the wood stoves burnin' in the valley.

                      C
And I know that I am homeward bound.

Ending:
   G   *C*
And, I know that I am homeward bound.

   G   *C*   *F*   *C*
And, I know that I am homeward bound ... homeward bound.

Hamilton Service Center, old Route 7 (Colonial Highway), Hamilton, VA.

Natural Mercantile, nearby.

Historic building, Hamilton, VA.

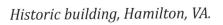

3

7 West Through The Blue Ridge

By Clare Reed c 1995

I'm head-ed sev-en west through the Blue Ridge. I'm watch-ing
still serv-ing break-fast at the Pine Grove. And that the

fall leaves fall-ing town to town. I smell the wood stoves burn-ing in the
Blue-mont Fair is com-ing 'round. I see the sun is set-ting o'er the

val-ley. And I know that I am home-ward bound. I know they're
Blue Ridge. No pret-tier sight can be found

Route 7 between Purcellville and Berryville, VA.

Purcellville Family Restaurant, old Route 7
(Main Street).

From the other direction. Come on in!

The White Palace, Main Street, Purcellville.

Across the street from the White Palace.

"Forever Yours"

Words and Music by Clare Reed March 5, 1996

Forever Yours

                 G   **D**

Verse 1. If there was only one dream that I could dream of,

                 G   **C**   **D**

If there was only one wish that I could have,

               G   **C**   **Am7**

I would dream that I am always loving you, love.

                  G   **D**   **G**

And I would wish that you would always love me too.

G   **C**   **D**   **G**

Chorus: Forever Yours, love. I'll be yours for-ev-er.

          C   **D**   **G**

I will love you 'til the mountains and seas are one again.

          C   **D**   **G**

Forever Yours, love. I'll be yours for-ev-er.

          C   **D**   **G**

I will love you 'til we both go home again.

                  G   **D**

Verse 2: There are times when I think - that you don't love me.

               G   **C**   **D**

There are times when I feel - that I don't care.

                  G   **C**   **Am7**

But there are times when I know – that you feel the same way too.

               G   **D**   **G**

Then I know that - I'm still in love with you. <u>**"Chorus"**</u>

            G   **D**

Verse 3: When I listen to my heart, it says "I love you".

         G   **C**   **D**

And, I know that deep inside - you love me too.

                 G   **C**   **Am7**

Let's renew our promises today - to love, honor and obey.

           G   **D**   **G**

And to spend our lives together -Two as One. <u>**"Chorus"**</u>

by Clare Reed 03/05/1996

10

Dental Building, just north of Main Street (old Route 7), Purcellville, VA.

Nichols Hardware, across the street, Purcellville.

Purcellville Marketplace, just off Main Street.

Purcellville Marketplace lunch counter.

Forever Yours

Clare Reed 1996

Bethany United Methodist Church, West Main Street (old Route 7), Purcellville.

The overpass where old Route 7 crosses new Route 7, going to Round Hill.

Sign for the historic Weona Villa motel between Purcellville and Round Hill. Dorothy and Bob Harper built it in 1954 and ran it until 2007, when Bob died. It then closed, but Dorothy maintained it as though it would receive guests at any time until 2017 when she passed away.

14

"Jesus, I Love You Most Of All"

Words and Music by Clare Reed July 22, 1996

Inspired by Ruth G. Barton, Grayson, GA

JESUS, I LOVE YOU MOST OF ALL

CHORUS: E

JESUS, I LOVE YOU MOST OF ALL

EVEN MORE THAN MY FAVORITE TIME
                        B7
WHEN SUM-MER TURNS TO FALL…………
E   E
HOW I LOVE TO HEAR THE WHIPPORWILLS CALL
      A   B7   E
BUT JESUS, I LOVE YOU MOST OF ALL.

VERSE 1:   A   E
I LOVE SUMMERTIME AND WINTERTIME AND FLOWERS IN THE SPRING.
         A   B7
I LOVE PONY TAILS AND COTTON TAILS AND BIRDS ON THE WING. BUT…
CHORUS

VERSE 2:   A   E
I LOVE COTTON CANDY, BABY RUTHS, AND GOLDYLOCKS WITH CREAM.
         A
I LOVE ROLLER COASTERS, FARRIS WHEELS,
    B7
AND MERRY-GO-ROUNDS WITH SWINGS! BUT…
 CHORUS

VERSE 3:   A   E
I LOVE ROCK AND ROLL, THINGS OF OLD AND WATCHING BABIES CRAWL
         A
I LOVE PEANUT BUTTER, CHOCOLATE COVERED,
    B7
AND THE COLORS IN THE FALL BUT…
CHORUS

ENDING: A   D   F#m
AND, JESUS, I LOVE YOU MORE THAN ALL THE STARS ABOVE.
   A   B   E
JESUS, I LOVE YOU MOST OF ALL!

(REPEAT ENDING)

by Clare Reed 07/22/1996
Inspired by Ruth G. Barton, Grayson, GA

*Tammy's Diner in Round Hill,
VA, on Route 7 Business.*

Round Hill Auto Service.

*West Loudoun Repair
in Round Hill.*

Jesus, I Love You Most Of All

Inspired by Ruth G. Barton

Clare Reed 1996

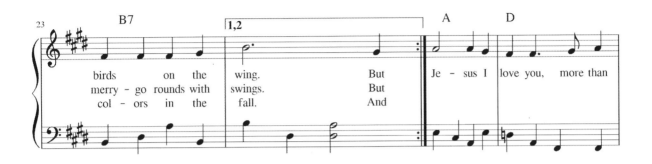

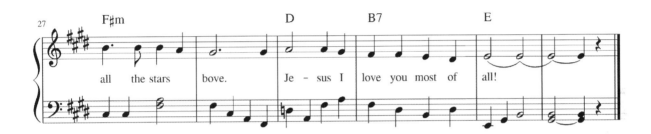

Bethany United Methodist Church, West Main Street (old Route 7), Purcellville.

Downtown Round Hill, on old Route 7. At the corner is Savoir Fare Restaurant, once a theater, with the Round Hill United Methodist Church in the background.

Another view of Savoir Fare.

Cruising through Round Hill.

"Just A Step Away"

Words and Music by Clare Reed August 7, 1992

JUST A STEP AWAY

VERSE:

G   D
JESUS, LOOK INTO MY HEART AND TELL ME WHAT YOU SEE.
                                                  G
IS THERE LOVE AND JOY AND PEACE, DEEP INSIDE OF ME?
 G   G7
AM I FOLLOWING THE BLUEPRINT
              C   Am
THAT MY LIFE IS MEANT TO BE?
        D   C   G
AM I PLEASING IN YOUR EYES, OR AM I JUST A STEP AWAY?

CHORUS:

G   C   G
AM I JUST A STEP AWAY FROM YOU AND ETERNITY?
        D   G   G7
FROM LOVE AND JOY AND PURITY.
                        C   G
AM I JUST A STEP AWAY FROM ALL I WAS MEANT TO BE?
        D   C   G
LORD, TELL ME PLEASE. AM I JUST A STEP AWAY?

REPEAT VERSE/CHORUS:
                        D   C   G
2ND TIME: LORD TELL ME PLEASE. AM I JUST A STEP AWAY?
                        D   C   G
3RD TIME: LORD TELL ME PLEASE. AM I JUST- A STEP - AWAY?
SLOWLY

by Clare Reed 08/07/1992
22

This is a particularly important place to bluegrass musicians – the Old Furniture Factory, home of the Round Hill Bluegrass Jam. Musicians met on the last Friday of each month to play together for about 14 years. Folding chairs were set up for a small audience, and there were folding tables for snacks or dinners catered by Savoir Fare across the street. Savoir Fare bought the building. The jams are not going on now while the building is being renovated, but who knows what the future holds?

Clare's music is a favorite at the Round Hill jam and the Loudoun County Bluegrass Association.

Loudoun County Bluegrass Association,
with Ted, Shreve, Gary, Bruce, Sue, John, Clare, Rich, Lacy, and Jerry

Just A Step Away

Clare Reed 1992

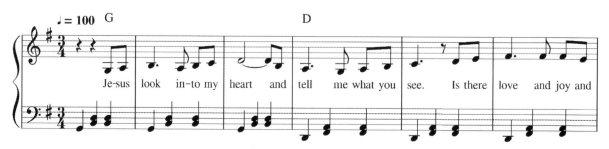

Je-sus look in-to my heart and tell me what you see. Is there love and joy and

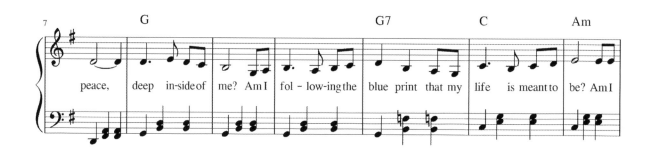

peace, deep in-side of me? Am I fol – low-ing the blue print that my life is meant to be? Am I

plea – sing in your eyes. Or am I just a step a – way? Am I just a step a – way from
(Chorus)

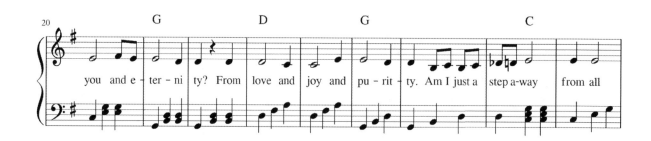

you and e – ter – ni ty? From love and joy and pu – rit – ty. Am I just a step a-way from all

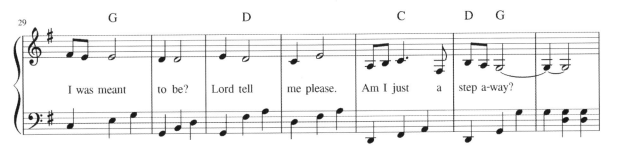

I was meant — to be? Lord tell — me please. Am I just a step a-way?

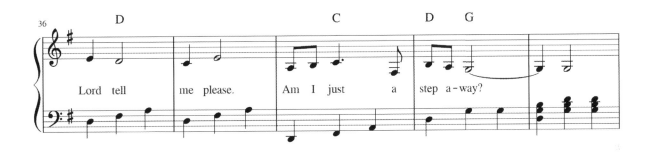

Lord tell — me please. Am I just a step a-way?

Lord tell — me please. Am I just a step a-way?

Ending
Repeat slowly

Clare Reed.

On the west side of Mt. Weather, heading toward Pine Grove and Berryville, VA.

The Horseshoe Curve Restaurant, on the steep and curvy Pine Grove road off Route 7.

Pine Grove Restaurant, Pine Grove, VA. On the Pine Grove Road off Route 7.

"Only Yesterday"

Words and Music by Clare Reed August 14, 1994

Only Yesterday

Verse 1:

G   D   G

It was Only Yesterday, I first heard you say, I love you.

           D   G G7

Wasn't it yesterday, I answered back, I love you too.

                  C   D   G D Em

How could time have gone by so fast, it just can't be.

                  C   D   G

Have we forgotten that, the love we had, was Only Yesterday.

Chorus:

         C   D   G

Yesterday, when dreams were young and bold.

                    C   D

Never dreaming how they would unfold.

        C D   G D Em

Always looking for that sunny day.

             C   D   G

Can't believe it was Only Yesterday.

Verse 2:

G   D   G

It was Only Yesterday, when we heard our first baby cry.

           D   G G7

Wasn't it yesterday, we laughed until we almost cried.

         C   D   G D Em

It was a time when dreams were changing day by day.

         C   D   G

Can't be-lieve that when, we made those dreams, it was Only Yesterday.

Chorus

Verse 3:

G   D   G

It was Only Yesterday, that I heard you say, I love you.

           D   G G7

It was Only Yesterday, I answered back, I love you too.

             C   D   G D Em

Although time has passed, our love has grown, how can it be.

             C   D   G

That we're still in love, just as though, it was Only Yesterday. **Chorus**

by Clare Reed 08/14/1994

28

Only Yesterday

by Clare Reed 1994

Where It Started

Let's shift gears here – this isn't Route 7, or the Blue Ridge. This is Clare's childhood home in Cincinnati, OH. It's where she started her musical path, singing on the swing in the back yard. "Pickles and Bubblegum" is a happy reminiscence of those times.

It's empty now, but there were three swings on the swingset! The park behind it was a cornfield.

"Pickles and Bubblegum"

Words and Music by Clare Reed 1997

Pickles and Bubblegum

```
                     C                    F              C
Verse 1:  Pickles and Bubblegum, Salt Shakers and Ice.
                     C                        G7
          These are memories of long ago.
                     C                              F            C
          Standin' in the kitchen watchin' snow flakes fall outside.
                     C           G7        C
          These are memories of long ago.
                     C            F         C
Chorus:   And they take me way back, way, way, back.
                   C        F       C
          Back to a time long ago oh oh.
                   C              F          C
          And they take me way back, way on back.
                 G7                      C
          Back to a time when I was young.
                     C                              F              C
Verse 2:  Sittin' on the big front porch watchin' rain drops fall.
                     C                        G7
          Hidin' underneath our fort of chairs.
                     C                          F            C
          Laughin' and a gigglin' when we'd hear the thunder roar.
                     C            G7            C
          Screamin' when we hear the thunder clap.
                     C            F         C
Chorus:   And they take me way back, way, way  back.
                   C        F       C
          Back to a time long ago oh oh.
                   C              F          C
          And they take me way back, way on back.
                 G7                      C
          Back to a time when I was young.
```

34

                   C   F   C

Verse 3: Playin' Jacks and Paper Dolls with the kids next door.

                   C   G7

Jumpin' rope with skate keys 'round our necks.

                   C   F   C

Playin' Hide & Seek and hollerin' out Olle Um Cum Free.

                   C   G7   C

Wonderin' which kid would come in last.

                   C   F   C

Chorus: And they take me way back, way, way back.

                   C   F   C

Back to a time long ago oh oh.

                   C   F   C

And they take me way back, way on back.

                G7   C

Back to a time when I was young.

Ending: C   F   C

Verse 1: Pickles and Bubblegum, Salt Shakers and Ice.

                   C   G7

These are memories of long ago.

                   C   F   C

Standin' in the kitchen watchin' snow flakes fall outside.

                   C   G7   C

These are memories of long ago.

                   C   F   C

Chorus: And they take me way back, way, way back.

                   C   F   C

Back to a time long ago oh oh.

                   C   F   C

And they take me way back, way on back.

Back to a time when I was young. (X2)

by Clare Reed 1997

Pickles and Bubblegum

Clare Reed 1997

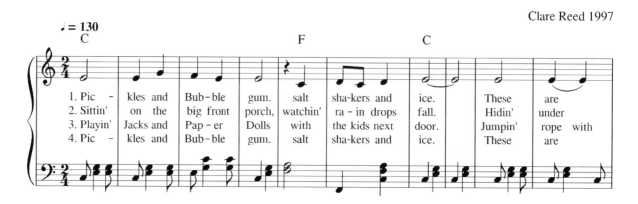

long a - go.
thun-der clap.
come in last.
long a - go.
(Chorus) And they take me way back, way

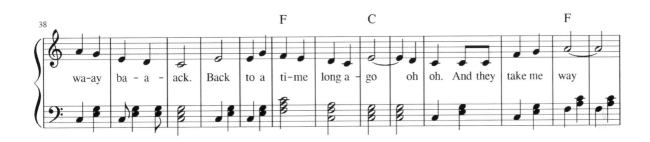

wa-ay ba-a-ack. Back to a ti-me long a-go oh oh. And they take me way

back, way o-n ba-a ack. Back to a time when I was young.

Downtown Berryville.

*The Ice Cream stand, where old Route 7
joins new Route 7 at Berryville, VA.*

B & O Train Station, Winchester, VA.

Judge John Handley of Scranton, PA left $250,000 in his will to " . . open a Public Library for the free use of the people of the city of Winchester forever." The Handley Library opened in 1913 at a cost of $233,230.28 for the building and furnishings. An addition to the building in was completed in1979.

Antebellum mansion at the corner of West Piccadilly and North Braddock streets was General Sherman's headquarters during part of the Civil War. The World's Largest Apple had been a parade float in the 1970s.

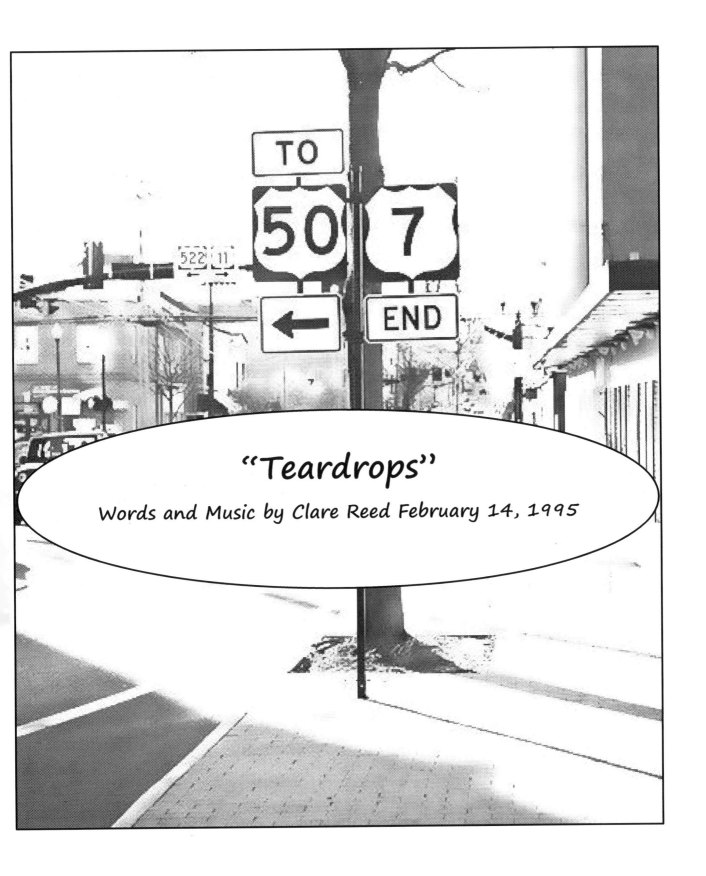

"Teardrops"

Words and Music by Clare Reed February 14, 1995

Teardrops

Chorus:
                       G   D   G

Chorus: Teardrops, gently falling. Teardrops - from my eyes.

                          C

Teardrops that you cause me

                     D   G

Every time you break this heart of mine.

                  G   D

Verse 1. You can't take away the sunshine on a bright and sunny day.

                                          G

You can't take away the stars on a moonlit night.

                                 C

But, you can take away my laughter when my heart is filled with joy.

                    D   G

And you can take away these Teardrops from my eyes.

Chorus

                  G   D

Verse 2. Bring me sweetness in the morning. Bring me laughter in the night.

                                 G

Bring me tenderness in your loving arms.

                                 C

Bring me sunshine in your eyes on a dark and cloudy day.

                  D   G

And you'll take away these Teardrops from my eyes.

Chorus

                  G   C

Bridge: Take them away, Take them away.

                    D   G

Please take away these Teardrops from my eyes.

                                C

Take them away, Oh, Take them away.

                D   G

Please take away these Teardrops from my eyes.

                  G   D   G

Chorus: Teardrops gently falling. Teardrops - from my eyes.

                          C

Teardrops that you cause me

                     D   G

Every time you break this heart of mine.

40

by Clare Reed 02/14/1995

Teardrops

Clare Reed 1995

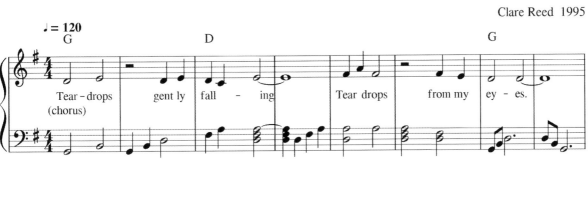

Tear - drops gently fall - ing Tear drops from my ey - es.
(chorus)

Tear drops that you cause me. Ev-ery ti - ime you break this heart of

mine. 1.You can't take a-way the sun-shine on a
2.Bring me sweet - ness in the morn-ing. Bring me

bright and sun - ny day. You can't take a-way the stars on a moon - lit
laugh - ter the night. Bring me ten - der-ness in your lov - ing

fro-om my ey – es. Tear drops that you cause me.

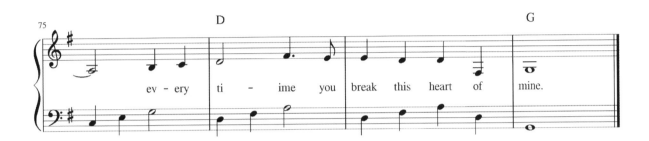

ev – ery ti – ime you break this heart of mine.

The George Washington Hotel in Winchester, VA. Completed in 1924, it was intended to serve passengers from the nearby B & O train station.

Piccadilly's Public House and Restaurant, originally a grocery warehouse near the train station.

Well, this really is the end of Route 7! Thank you, from all of us who love Clare's music and the northern Blue Ridge, for joining this journey of music and memories -

7 West Through The Blue Ridge!